To Pam, the love of my life.

I write my Introduction to this book dedicated to the love of my wife Pamela.
I wrote this book between 1989 and 1991 while on Her Majesty's Pleasure (H.M.P.)
I release this book now as Pamela has become seriously ill and I pray every day for that miracle.
I met Jesus while in prison in 1989 as I was in a dark place and I saw the light.
People have asked what was Jesus doing in prison? I replied "Saving me" and others in them dark places.
So I ask all my Jesus friends out there and others. Say a prayer for Pam.
God bless us all.
From the heart of Jeff Astler

Lady of Camelot

The knights of past, these men once bold
They'd carry their lance for a maiden to hold
My lance, my lady, I'll give to you,
Beautiful maiden of eyes so true
Horses of white and fields so green
Camelot, my lady, you have seen
When men did bow beneath your feet
And all stood still within the street
Centuries have gone and ages have passed
But my lady of Camelot, she will last
A knight of the table I may not be
But I hold my lance for all to see
So like those knights of once so bold
I have my maiden and mine to hold!

Above the Rest

Don't let life hold you down,
You're nobody's puppet, you're nobody's clown,
Stand up straight, yes, you out there,
Their wonderful mother, filled with care,
Out of all the women I've had to know,
It's you, my darling, that makes me glow,
For all the children you've given me,
You're above the rest, so let you see,
Life is cruel, and I should know,
I've felt the pain, I've cried the woe,
But I stand strong, because I love you,
For your motherly touch, and the things you do,
So you listen, my eternal mate,
You're above the rest, so stand up straight.

Angel of Love!

When God made you he broke the mould
Then called the angels and they were told
"This love of life I give to you
"Because She's a reflection of what I do
"She has the kindness and the cure
"To make one man's heart totally pure"
A gift from God he gave to me
His angel of love to set me free
So with this love from up above
She cured my heart and showed me love
So I thank God for my Gift
My angel in you who gives me lift
You give me rise the eternal way
And I thank God you were born that day!

Chilling Cold

The coldness grips the chilling night,
I want you near, to hold me tight,
To keep the cold outside my mind,
Away from the blizzard that makes me blind,
Shelter my love from this painful freeze,
Just come to my heart, and warm with ease,
Release your heat, my need I've felt,
Bring the thaw of my coldness to melt,
Let me love, be warm again,
Without this solitude, without this pain,
Come to me, with your warming light,
And touch my heart, and let me feel bright,
Banish this loneliness from my cell,
Of which is of my heart, is what I tell,
The story of a man, of the chilling cold,
But has an angel, who's made from gold,
So I'll close my eyes, on this cold night,
And there you are, so I'm alright.

Crest of Love

As the many moons within a sky,
Like the crests of love within your eye,
Venus, Jupiter, and the galaxies too,
All hold stars, just for you.
Your starlight wonder fills the night,
To a perfect passage, to do things right,
The Milky Way, bows down to you,
Because of the loving things that you do,
So my love, my life, you tell no lie,
You hold the answers within your eye,
My universe with you has no set time,
So stay forever, and please be mine!!

Cuddle

When I'm alone, and afraid at night,
Without your arms to hold me tight,
I close my eyes, I dream of you,
Holding me tight, as you do,
Then the fears, that are wrapped inside,
Find a corner, to run and hide,
And in my heart, out comes the band,
With your arms around me, while touching my
hand,
While in the corner, sits poor old fear,
Knowing you're close, so it can't come near,
So of my dreams, of while apart,
Cuddle me close within your heart!

Cupid

I have a story that's never been told
Not from the young, and not from the old,
It's the story of love, and I played a part,
Like cupid's bow I was his dart,
Shot from love through the sky,
Searching the heavens before I die.
This love I see is well out there,
Surrounded by beauty and surrounded with care,
My dart of love did land on you,
Because, of them all, you've stayed true.
So Cupid, Cupid, let it be,
That my golden angel has eyes for me,
Then, cupid, my friend, you may take your dart,
Because I'm laid to rest within her heart!!!

Eighty-Five

When we met in eighty-five
A destined love to survive
Roads of many we have trod
Without a staff, without a rod
Lonely nights within our pain
Like souls so lost in the rain
But, my baby, do not fear
I send protection of one dear
My angels of love come to you
Through my prayers to you know who
This power of strength within my mind
Knowing he's loving you, so gentle, so kind,
He gave us birth of our pure three
And we owe so much to the man called thee
So my darling the time's so near
Forget the worry and forget the fear
God's on the left and I'm on the right
So between us we'll hold you tight!

Lady of Camelot

The knights of past, these men once bold
They'd carry their lance for a maiden to hold
My lance, my lady, I'll give to you,
Beautiful maiden of eyes so true
Horses of white and fields so green
Camelot, my lady, you have seen
When men did bow beneath your feet
And all stood still within the street
Centuries have gone and ages have passed
But my lady of Camelot, she will last
A knight of the table I may not be
But I hold my lance for all to see
So like those knights of once so bold
I have my maiden and mine to hold!

Flames of Desire

Beneath the earth a red hot fire
Flames of love for my desire
Satan's home for poor lost souls
Who've lost their God and lost their goals
Desire my love, can't you tell
I'd quench those flames in burning hell
If a mistake and I went there
I'd fight for love with tender care
Shout to the heavens, I'd scream your name
And in my heart I know you came
To the home of love that's you and me
And they can't part us for eternity
So I'd leave the fires of burning hell
To the souls so bad that they have fell
And wings we'll make of feathers eleven,
Joined together we'll fly to heaven
And right across the golden gate
I'll put a plaque for my best mate
Upon the sign it will just say
"I'll love you, Pam, more every day!"

Flood

This lady I met, some years ago,
Told me her life was full of woe,
So within myself, I knew it was me,
To grab her heart, to let her see,
I'll flood her, with so much love,
As God did the earth, from the heavens above,
So my love, I'll build this Ark,
To ride the flood, to end the dark,
And when we settle, upon this land,
God will help us, within his hand,
So my lady, from years ago,
I'll love you to death, and kill your woe!

Heavenly Door

As the wind blows, outside my cage,
The rushing gale of all my rage,
Silence of fear, I hold within,
Knowing I'm paying for all my Sin,
The Sins of life, I had before,
Until you opened my heavenly Door,
This door you've seen, within your mind,
Where winds are calm, and gales are kind,
No starving mouths, room for all,
It's within your heart, though yet so small,
You've given me, while I'm in your cage,
Your heavenly love, to still my rage,
Memories of your love so true,
You still the wind, make my dark sky blue.

Heaven's Train

Within this world and when we start
You're given a soul and given a heart
The soul is there until we die
But upon which plain will it lie?
Is it the one below the earth,
Of no loving and no worth?
Or is it heaven, too far out
For lost souls to hear our shout?
Look down there you foolish thing
See what our love can truly bring
I have my love, she has my heart
She gave my life a soulful start
So when you live remember this
Our heaven's train, please don't miss
Book your ticket, book it now,
Ask your heart, it'll tell you how
Don't wander around and be too late
Because I've got my love and she's my mate!

I do swear!
The future we hold but yet to see
But I know it belongs to you and me
This love I wear bears your name
Filled with gold in a hall of fame
This kind of future is clear as day
Because along my heart you paved your way
Scattering seeds sown with care
Showing such love of mortals rare
So yes, my love, this feeling felt,
Beneath your heart I have knelt
I kneel to you my Royal Queen
Because of this future I have seen
So God's my judge, and I do swear
I'll always love you, and I'll always care!

I Promise

The roaring sound from up above,
As the gates will open to our new found love,
Angels will sit upon their cloud,
To witness this love we've made so proud,
The skies will twirl, they'll dance our tune,
Of skipping stones across the moon,
The birds will swim, the fish will fly,
And they'll be beams of love within the sky.
Time will stop to take a look,
At this written love within the book,
And you I promise as we met was fate,
This will happen when we pass the gate!!!

Kingdom of Love

The Kingdom of Love I hold for you
Fields of green and skies so blue
People may ask "Where is this place?
The land forgotten without a trace?"
It's in your heart, I will reply
They'll laugh and scoff and say I lie
"But No," I'll say, "How you dare,
Because, with my lady, we are there"
So open your heart and let it see
The power of love when it's free
I can prove that we are there
The way we love, the way we care,
But most play blind to this part
Because they have no love to open the heart
I'm just glad for you and me
That God touched us and we are free
So the Kingdom of Love I'll hold for you
Because you're so pure and, yes, so true!

Lady of Heaven

My link with God has come through you,
Because of my belief that all that's true,
They say that God is of the male,
But nobody's returned, to tell the tale,
This love you give me, it gives me sight,
My lady of heaven, my heart's delight,
God is one of many things,
Because to my life, it's you it brings,
So I'll not say that God's a male,
To no other idol to hail,
But in my thoughts, the picture true,
That God's a spirit, and it's in you,
Love and tenderness is the Spirit within,
To start my life, to love, to begin,
So my link with God, you can see is true,
Because of my belief, and my love for you!

Light of Love

The freedom of love was given to me
And I'll show them when I'm free
I'll show you things to gladden your heart
Love your feelings and play the part
Take to love to a different high
Past the clouds and past the sky
We'll touch the bottom of Ocean's blue
Just to show my love is true
I'd touch the stars in the night
To show you love, to show the light
The light of love which I have seen
And through barriers no-one's been
God's my judge to this sight
He gave me you, you are my light
So with this poem I do end
I'll honour and love and always defend!

Lover's Hand

As the time approaches, very soon,
We'll walk together, under the moon,
Perfect lovers, hand in hand,
Through the dark, and across this land,
Passing by the fields of night,
Been shown the way, beneath our moonlight,
As we are strolling, I'll stop and say,
I'll love you for eternity, is that OK?
While praying your answer, you give to me,
Tells my soul, whether he's totally free,
My prayer is answered, I hear your reply,
I'll love you for eternity, until I die,
So thank-you, lover, for holding my hand,
And freeing my soul, across this land.

Love's a drug!!
Closing my eyes and picturing you
As my mind's within the Zoo
No power on earth can stop my thought
Because the strength of love we've been taught
No walls, no gates, no fences, no key
Can stop our love and they can see
Love, this unstoppable word
Pierces anything when it's heard
You can't control this boiling gush
It's a drug and you get a rush
When you're close I'm on a high
Like soaring birds within the sky
It's not a drug bought on the street
It's a love when two people meet
Yes, my darling, as you and I
You hold my love upon a high!!!

Magical Lady

The lights are out, the sounds are grooving,
Landings still, no, servants moving,
The sounds of music, echo the cell,
Of every con, in his private hell,
No keys are swinging, the night is still,
But through my thoughts, my heart you fill,
Your love pours in, and spills the rim,
Through the walls, of prison grim,
Magical lady, you come to me,
And mend my heart, and set me free,
So with this thought, I'll close to end,
You are my lover, and you're my friend!

Miss

This lonely feeling, of this my stage,
Is written my missing, on every page,
My heart is caged, within this crime,
The haunting feeling of doing time,
But, I feel, the day so near,
That I'll hold you close, and lose my fear,
This fear that rises, and hurts so much,
Because I'm in a cage, and I can't touch,
So on with my missing, of you each day,
And with my thoughts, I'll sit and pray,
My prayer to God, goes like this,
Truly my love, it's you I miss.

My Butterfly

The wings of my butterfly are held with grace,
Woven with love, from a golden lace,
Time was taken, and that is true,
As God took time, when he made you,
He threaded a heart into a perfect frame,
Because you and loveliness are just the same,
Then moulded your soul from a golden ring,
And ordered his angels to start to sing,
The song they sang was of a butterfly,
Of golden wings, who couldn't die,
It's life like yours, is truly right,
Because you're so beautiful, to my sight!

My Dream

As of my feelings you own so much,
With your flowing smile, and your faithful touch,
Your laughter lifts, to brighten my day,
And your eye's so close to where I lay,
I feel your wonder, within my jail,
The bars, the keys, they've come to fail,
They can't stop, for what I seem,
Because I'm with you, within my dream,
My dream of love, of what you are,
This shooting angel, of above so far,
You come to me, within my night,
To lighten my darkness, to move my fright,
Thank-you angel, for being there,
For loving my dreams,
And giving me care,
So when asleep within my night,
Come on in, and hold me tight!

My Temple

Within my heart, I hold this power,
My temple to heaven, my love, the tower,
And at the top, your life I grasp,
Then to our maker, I will ask,
"If life should stop, God, promise me,
"That within your heaven, mine she'll be,
"I've built this temple, to honour you,
"Because of her heart, you gave me true,
"I've fought with fire, I've battled hell,
"And of your goodness, I do to tell,
"So may I request, one favour from you,
"Fit our love, in your temple too,
"That when we leave, our turn to die,
"We'll be within your house within the sky."

My Winds

With the blowing winds across this moor
Of the silent steps upon the floor
My heart, my soul you gave to me
The day we met the day I see
My love for you as a howling gale
Of my true love, I tell this tale
My winds of love I send to you
Because I love you, because you're true
Upon your heart these winds will blow
To show how much you make me glow
So when you hear the breeze outside
You'll know my love will be your guide
So with my winds I will just say
I'll love you more and more each day!!

Nice to Dream

To my love, my love, I dream
Wandering thoughts to one so bold
Maker of love maker of men
Whether young love or whether so old.

Chorus: So, maker of life, so maker so seem?
In our love, it's nice to dream.

The key to life we may never see
Or the lock to mayhem will never do
But it's nice to dream, just you and me
Because we're not a god, who says who.

Prayer

As we close our eyes, to rest our mind,
To sleep the night, of peace so kind,
We have our prayer, to god above,
Surround us all, with living love,
My prayer for you, is such a strength,
It gets to heaven, at any length,
I have the number, I'm on that line,
And then He answers, you're doing fine,
So before I close, to sleep at night,
I say my prayers, for Him to right.
To keep you safe, to keep you well,
Until I'm released, from Satan's Hell.

Precious Lady

These loving times, you've given me,
Have cleansed my heart, without a fee,
No money on earth, can you pay,
For this kind of loving, you've shown this way.
Priceless feelings are so antique,
From my precious lady, I found to seek,
God gave you love, a joyful gift,
That warms my mind, and my heart does lift,
To heights of pleasure. Never climbed before,
As you knocked on my heart, and opened my
door,
So, my precious lady, of my heart, key,
Thank-you, darling, for loving me!

Silence of Love

The silence of love the angels sing
I'll marry this girl, she'll wear my ring
Tunes will play within the dark
And innocent children will play the harp
Birds will find a golden song
To make things right that have been so wrong
God will send the signs to me
And make the believer truly see
Will you love the thought so true
That, my angel, I'll marry you
If my worth is paid in gold
Give your love so I can hold
And I'll tell God this feeling mine
That I'll love her till the end of time!

Stairway to Heaven

If I go to Heaven, and you're not there,
I'll write your name, on the golden stair
For all the world, to know and see,
That you, my love, belong to me.
I'll give saint Peter back his wings,
And that golden halo, of lovely things,
Just to prove, my love's still true,
I'll come to Hell, to be with you.

Surrounded

The mist is rising, I can see the dawn,
I've woken from sleep, to feel the morn,
Life is pumping, through my soul,
As I clamber, from this hole,
And upon this earth, I can see,
That you were born, to set me free,
As you walk, you move the air,
Filling the atmosphere with so much care,
So I'm not frightened to leave this hole,
Because I know you love me, you've told my soul,
And with you, and God above,
I know I'm surrounded, with so much love!

They

The pain they've given, throughout the years,
Ones of loss and lonely tears,
This given to me, to justify,
But within my heart, I only cry,
My drops of sadness, is my need to lose,
Upon my heart, they've left their bruise,
This mark they've left, by using you,
The weapon they have, because my love so true,
They couldn't hurt me, before they've tried,
So they take you away and put me inside,
Now the pain hits my heart,
They've broken my strength, while we're apart,
But soon the day they lose their hold,
Because my love for you is growing bold,
So I'll sit in here, and I'll just wait,
Until the calendar shows my date,
And when that time comes to stay,
I'll show you love my special way,
So if they think they've won again,
My love for you weighs out their pain,
Sentence of crime, I cannot see,
Because within your love, they can't have me!

Time With No Reward

Gangland gangsters they have been
Sometimes ruthless, sometimes mean,
Stand up people who have the might
But within this system they have no right
Ronnie and Reggie, that's the name,
Stuck in the system on that fame
Enough, enough, set them free
They've paid for their crimes so let them be
Alone a lifetime with their thought
Of pain and anguish the system's taught
Men once of fear, now once of knowledge
They've seen the school they learnt in college
Those prisons of sin, your morals, your teacher
Learnt from love, of our early preacher
So Ronnie and Reggie, never give in,
You've passed your crime, you've paid for your
sin!

Woman So Kind

In this pit, my hell I lie,
As lonely darkness passes by,
Outside my walls, I hold no fear,
Because my heart, you touch me dear,
The shackled sound, of thoughts of flight,
You're in my presence, you hold me tight.
This lonely mist, within my cell,
Because it's a dream, and I'm in hell,
But no hot coals, nor even fire,
Can quench my thirst, for your desire,
So with my hell, within my mind,
I'll picture you, my woman so kind.

Wonders

The wonders of life, they are seven,
Built to last and made in heaven,
But I'm sure I have number eight,
And she's my lover and my best mate,
Made from love just you and I,
Like angels from heaven just flying by,
We have touched the wings of love,
Like releasing the bird, the pure white dove,
The Ark was built to save the day,
As you did when you came my way,
So, Wonders of Life, you're not seven,
Because she's eight and made in heaven!

Words

My words of love, I write so plain,
As from my heart I try to explain,
The sights of beauty, you've shown me there,
Filled with wonders, and sowed with care.
I've seen love, from its birth,
As God did make our Mother Earth,
Fantasies or reality, or maybe a dream,
But within my heart, I have seen,
Glorious lovers, as you and I,
With a fondness that will never die,
So with all my words, I write so true,
As with every sentence, I love you!!!

Your Garden!
The land of heaven I hold for you
And you know my love I know you do
Heaven's not made of what it seems
It's my fantasy within my dreams
The Garden of Eden, it's all there
My words of love, I write so plain,
As from my heart I try to explain,
The sights of beauty, you've shown me there,
Filled with wonders, and sowed with care.
I've seen love, from its birth,
As God did make our Mother Earth,
Fantasies or reality, or maybe a dream,
But within my heart, I have seen,
Glorious lovers, as you and I,
With a fondness that will never die,
So with all my words, I write so true,
As with every sentence, I love you!!!

But without the Serpent who destroyed care
And in its place I've put my love
In the form of a white pure Dove
So when we walk in our heaven's dream
We've made our garden of what we've seen
I don't want the knowledge of the Tree of Life
But I pray to God you'll be my wife
Because if first upon this land
We'd have spread love hand in hand

Final Conclusion

The final conclusion is here to stay
Because I've written a different way,
I've spoken the words, for the just,
And of this conclusion, which is a must,
The must of right, the touch of love,
Plus the feelings of God above,
This conclusion of life is open to see,
Follow our hearts, and you will be,
A person of truth, a man of Correction,
Looking for lies and feeling deception,
But most of all, I'll have the gain,
Of a final Conclusion, without the pain.

21282621R00027

Printed in Great Britain
by Amazon